DENALI NATIONAL PARK AND PRESERVE

A TRUE BOOK

by

David Petersen

Children's Press®
A Division of Grolier Publishing

New York London Hong Kong Sydney
Danbury, Connecticut

For Liza Crockett

Reading Consultant
Linda Cornwell
Learning Resource Consultant
Indiana Department of
Education

Denali National Park and
Preserve is considered to be
one of the finest wilderness
regions in North America.

Library of Congress Cataloging-in-Publication Data

Petersen, David, 1946–
    Denali National Park and Preserve / by David Petersen.
        p.   cm.   —   (A true book)
    Includes index.
    Summary: Describes the landscape, wildlife and activities for visitors at
Alaska's Denali National Park.
    ISBN 0-516-20050-X (lib.bdg.)   ISBN 0-516-26096-0 (pbk.)
    1. Denali National Park and Preserve (Alaska)—Juvenile literature.
[1. Denali National Park and Preserve (Alaska)   2. National parks and
reserves.] I. Title. II. Series.
F912.M23P48   1996
917.98'3—dc20   96-1574
                                                                   CIP
                                                                   AC

Contents

4

Denali National Park and Preserve

Denali National Park and Preserve is one of the richest wildlife regions in North America. It is also one of the most beautiful places on Earth.

The park stretches across six million acres (2.4 million hectares) of Alaska, the

Arctic Circle

Denali National
Park and Preserve

largest state in the United
States. It lies just 200 miles
(322 kilometers) south of the
Arctic Circle. Winters there
are very cold, with a lot of
snow. The average January
temperature is -7 degrees
Fahrenheit (-22 degrees

Celsius). So, although Denali is open year-round, most people visit the park during the summer months.

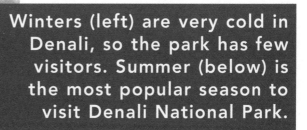

Winters (left) are very cold in Denali, so the park has few visitors. Summer (below) is the most popular season to visit Denali National Park.

Mount McKinley is the highest peak in North America.

Denali National Park takes its name from its biggest mountain. Denali is an Athabascan word that means "The Great One." The mountain called Denali is

8

the highest peak in North America. It rises 20,320 feet (6,190 meters) above sea level.

Outside Alaska, this majestic mountain is known as Mount McKinley. In 1917, when the park was established, it was called Mount McKinley National Park.

Since its earliest days as a national park, visitors have flocked there to explore.

President William McKinley

At that time, the United States government, led by President William McKinley, was concerned that human settlement and overhunting might wipe out the area's large animals. This national park was created to protect the wild animals that live there.

Then, in 1980, the park was enlarged to its present size, and its name was changed to Denali National Park and Preserve. Every year, more than 600,000 people visit Denali. Let's find out why so many people travel so far to visit such a remote and rugged place.

Near the park's entrance, visitors get a spectacular view of Mount McKinley.

Wildlife

Some visitors come to admire, photograph, and even climb Mount McKinley. But most people come to see the wildlife.

Throughout Denali, thousands of caribou roam free. The caribou is a large-antlered deer—a cousin of the European reindeer.

Caribou (above) are the North American versions of reindeer. Caribou roam free in Denali and often have close encounters with visitors (inset).

Moose (left) can be seen in abundance through-out Denali National Park and Preserve. Dall sheep (right) are hard to find because they live very high up in the mountains.

An even larger deer found at Denali is the moose—the largest deer in the world. The males weigh 1,500 pounds

(680 kg) and their antlers can grow up to 5 feet (1.5 m) wide!

Visitors also come to Denali in hopes of seeing Dall sheep. These big, snow-white cliff-dwellers bound gracefully over the icy mountain ridges they call home.

But the most popular animal in Denali is the mighty grizzly bear. Almost every day during the summer, grizzlies can be seen roaming along the park road.

Grizzly

Although newborn grizzlies are as tiny as puppies, they grow up to eight feet (2.4 m) long and weigh five hundred pounds (227 kg) or more. They have thick, woolly underfur that ranges in color from light tan to almost black.

Bears

The grizzly bear is the most dangerous mammal in North America. It is also the most magnificent.

Most grizzly bears try to avoid contact with people. But there have been occasions when grizzlies have attacked and killed humans.

Wolves are a common sight at Denali.

A few Denali visitors are
lucky enough to see wolves.
On moonlit nights, campers
often hear them howling.
    The sky above Denali
National Park and Preserve
belongs to the golden eagle,

the Alaska jay, and many other fascinating birds. In all, Denali is home to 159 species of birds and 37 kinds of mammals.

Nesting birds and curious bears are among the fascinating wildlife found throughout the park.

The Denali Shuttle

When visitors arrive at Savage River, 15 miles (24 km) inside Denali, they must park their cars and board shuttle buses. The bus fare is included in the price of park admission.

The absence of traffic on the park's single road makes it easy to see Denali's wildlife.

The shuttle buses stop often so visitors can enjoy Denali's breathtaking views. The one road that winds through Denali helps preserve the park's natural beauty by keeping traffic low.

The park is free of noise, air pollution, and traffic jams—disturbances that would scare animals away from the road.

A shuttle bus passes in each direction along the park road every 30 minutes, all day long. You can get off the bus almost anywhere and stop for as long as you wish. When you're ready to move on, just flag down the next bus going your way.

A High and Icy World

Denali National Park and Preserve lies along a chain of mountains called the Alaska Range. The Alaska Range was created between 2 million and 5 million years ago, when the land was pushed up by great pressure within the earth.

The mountains of the Alaska Range

Today, thick glaciers are still
a part of the Alaska Range.
Glaciers are huge slabs of ice
that form when more snow
falls in the winter than melts

during the summer. Over a very long time, the snow becomes compressed into a thick sheet of ice that flows slowly downhill.

The glaciers at Denali have existed for thousands of years.

Visitors can even explore Denali's glaciers.

As they move, glaciers gouge and carve the earth and rocks, changing the shape of the land. One of Denali's largest glaciers, Muldrow, is 35 miles (56 km) long and comes to within half a mile (.8 km) of the park road.

Three Life Zones

Despite its extreme cold, Denali is rich in plant life. Naturalists divide the park into three zones, according to the life forms that live in each one.

The first, and lowest, zone is called the taiga—a Russian word meaning "land of little sticks." Dense forests of spruce, aspen, poplar, birch, and larch

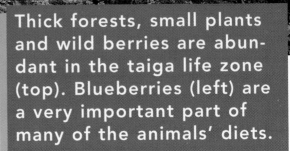

Thick forests, small plants and wild berries are abundant in the taiga life zone (top). Blueberries (left) are a very important part of many of the animals' diets.

trees grow on the taiga. Blueberries, cranberries, crowberries, and other wild shrubs are found beneath the trees.

Animals and birds visit the taiga in the autumn to enjoy its sweet treats. Grizzlies and black bears like to feast on these wild berries. The tiny fruits help the big bears to gain the weight they need for hibernation— their long winter sleep.

A grizzly bear munches on blueberries to prepare for its winter hibernation.

Above a certain point, the weather is too harsh for trees to grow. This point is called the timberline.

In Denali, the timberline occurs at about 2,800 feet (853 m). Here, taiga gives way to tundra—a hilly, almost treeless, world.

Trees do not grow above the timberline.

The word tundra comes from a Lapp word meaning "hill." Plants in the tundra are dwarfed by the short growing season, strong winds, deep snow, and intense cold.

Denali has two kinds of tundra. The park's second, or middle life zone, is called the moist tundra. Moist tundra begins just above the timberline. Thick growths of birch and willow are plentiful, and moose come in winter to eat

Fall colors brighten Denali's tundra (left). Although the tundra is very cold, small plants can be found there (right).

their nutritious twigs and bark. In summer, caribou enjoy the same plants.

The park's third, and highest life zone is the dry alpine tundra that starts at 3,400 feet (1,036 m). Alpine tundra supports only the smallest plant life, but most alpine plants produce flowers.

Small, flowering plants are able to grow in Denali's dry alpine tundra zone.

Even tiny flowers bring color to Denali's cold alpine tundra zone.

In June and July, Denali's alpine tundra zone is a shimmering sea of purple, white, and yellow flowers. Alaska's state flower, the forget-me-not, is just one of Denali's 430 kinds of plants.

34

Seeing Denali Safely

Since Denali is a wilderness, its weather, wildlife, and landscape can be unpredictable. Visitors must be extra careful. Remember that you must never try to pet or feed a wild animal. Animals— particularly bears and moose—are very dangerous. Cute little animals like squirrels can bite, too, and they sometimes carry diseases.

It's best to view Denali's wildlife—particularly curious baby animals—from the safety of your vehicle (left). Camping (above) can add to the enjoyment of visiting Denali.

To be sure you have a safe and enjoyable visit to Denali, make the Visitor Access Center your first stop. There, you can learn about campgrounds, backcountry hiking, wildlife watching, bus rides, and more. And don't miss the 15-minute park orientation program.

The Visitor Center (top) has a lot of park information available. Visitors especially enjoy the daily dog-sledding demonstration (left).

From the Visitor Access Center, it's just a 15-minute bus ride to the sled-dog kennels. There, park rangers give daily dog-sledding demonstrations.

Sled-Dogs

Sled-dogs are strong, hearty, and courageous. They have great endurance that allows them to pull their sleds over long distances. A sled-dog team can travel 20 to 40 miles (32 to 64 km) a day.

There are usually **three to eight dogs** in a sled-dog team. Each dog is hitched **one behind the other** to a long lead. Sometimes, two or more dogs are hitched **side by side.** The **lead dog takes commands from the** driver. The **driver walks or runs alongside** the sled, hopping on to the back of the sled every few minutes for a short ride.

Alaska's Iditarod Trail Sled-Dog Race is held every February. The race runs 1,100 miles (1,770 km) from Anchorage to Nome.

On Your Own Two Feet

Once you've become familiar with Denali, get off the bus and take a hike. You can hike alone or with your family and friends. Or you can join a ranger-guided walk.

Every day during the summer, rangers guide Denali Discovery hikes through the

Hiking is one of the best ways to see Denali (left). Rangers are available to educate and guide visitors (below).

park's many wonders. Sign up for Denali Discovery hikes at the Visitor Access Center.

Be A Denali Junior Ranger

Taking a Denali Discovery hike is the first step toward becoming a Denali Junior Ranger. To learn what else you must do to earn this honor, ask at the Visitor Access Center. Or, you can read about it in the park newspaper, the *Denali Alpenglow*.

Sunset over the Alaska Range is breathtaking.

Alaska's Denali National Park and Preserve is one of the most unspoiled and beautiful places on Earth. You'll never forget your visit.

43

To Find Out More

Here are some additional resources to help you learn more about Denali National Park and Preserve.

 **Books**

Crump, Donald J., ed. **Adventures in Your National Parks.** National Geographic, 1994.

Dunmire, Marj (Illus.). **National Parks of Alaska.** Pegasus Graphics, 1991.

Fradin, Dennis. **Alaska.** Children's Press, 1993.

Weber, Michael. **Our National Parks.** Millbrook Press, 1994.

 **Organizations**

Denali National Park
P.O. Box 9
Denali Park, AK 99755
907-683-2294

National Park Service
Office of Public Inquiries
P.O. Box 37127
Washington, DC 20013
202-208-4747

**Alaska Region
National Park Service**
2525 Gambell Street
Anchorage, AK 99503
907-257-2696

**National Parks and
Conservation Association**
1776 Massachusetts
  Avenue, NW
Washington, DC 20036
800-NAT-PARK
natparks@aol.com
npca@npca.org

Great Outdoor Recreation Pages (GORP)

*http://www.gorp.com/gorp/
resource/US_National_Park/
main.htm*

Information on hiking, fishing, boating, climate, places to stay, plant life, wildlife, and more.

National Park Foundation

CompuServe offers online maps, park products, special programs, a question-and-answer series, and in-depth information available by park name, state, region, or interest. From the main menu, select *Travel*, then *Where To Go*, then *Complete Guide to America's National Parks*.

National Park Service World Wide Web Server

http://www.nps.gov

Includes virtual tours, maps, and essays.

National Parks Magazine

editorial@npca.org

Focuses on the park system in general, as well as on individual sites.

Note: Many of the national parks have their own home pages on the World Wide Web. Do some exploring!

Important Words

Arctic Circle cold, icy area surrounding the North Pole

Athabascan language of the American Indians who live in the northernmost regions of North America

dense crowded together

kennel place where dogs are kept

Lapp person from northern Scandinavia

mammal warm-blooded animal that gives live birth and nurses its young; dogs, bears, whales, and humans are mammals

naturalist scientist who studies nature

orientation introduction to something new

shimmering glimmering or sparkling

Index

Meet the Author

David Petersen lives in a little cabin on a big mountain in Colorado and visits Alaska as often as possible. Mr. Petersen enjoys traveling and has visited each of the national parks about which he has written for Children's Press. Other titles he has written in the True Books series include: *Death Valley National Park, Bryce Canyon National Park,* and *Petrified Forest National Park.*